NIGHT WA

SOME POETRY BY PETER SCUPHAM

The Air Show
Selected Poems
Watching the Perseids
The Ark

PETER SCUPHAM

Night Watch

For Debra,
Peter Scupham 99

ANVIL PRESS POETRY

ACKNOWLEDGEMENTS

Poems have appeared in *Birdsuit, HQ, Oxford Poetry,*
PN Review and *The Rialto*

Published in Great Britain in 1999
by Anvil Press Poetry
Neptune House 70 Royal Hill London SE10 8RF

ISBN 0 85646 319 1

This book is published
with financial assistance from
The Arts Council of England

Set in Monotype Janson by Anvil
Printed in Great Britain
by The Cromwell Press Trowbridge Wilts

A catalogue record for this book
is available from The British Library

For Margaret

Contents

It's Good to Talk   11
A Victorian Way of Death, 1998   12
Arras: Easter 1998   13
Midi   15
Quick-Quick-Slow   16
Falling Downstairs   17
Uncle Walt   18
A Slice of Cake   19
Family Reunion   20
Parting   23
Crossing the Peak   24
The Northern Line

   1   BOARDING   25
   2   UNDER WAY   26
   3   JUNCTION   27
   4   OFF AGAIN   28
   5   BACK   29
   6   ST PANCRAS   30
   7   UNDERGROUND   31
   8   WATERLOO   32
   9   ENCOUNTER   33
  10   SOUTH   34
  11   TERMINUS   35

Night Watch   36
Night Kitchen   37
In the Picture   39
Nothing at All   40
A Trunk of Letters   41
In Camera   42
The Old Home   44
Lunch Out   46
The Letter   48
Trevail: Four Children & Summer   51
Kippford: A View from the Bridge   52

Lea Valley: My Son, My Father   53
Epithalamion   54
Song for Sophie   56
The Christmas Owl   57
Riches Heures du Duc de Berry   60
Kilvert's Winter: 1871   62
The Chairs   65
A. C. Benson Has a Restless Night   67
Augustus Hare Considers Another Ghost Story   69
The Healer of Sick Pearls   71
Name and Nature   74
This Late Tempest   75

Night Watch

It's Good to Talk

We should have heard less than this,
paid more attention to the lip-service
offered by mile on greying mile
of queasy combers, rufflets of wind
where oak bustles against oak.
Small particulars ebb and flow,

swirl in a shell's black plastic orifice:
that chamber where something died
and a ghost heart murmurs
'But it's good to talk.' Things in orbit,
swung wires, the stunted lattices
whose heads bristle with a light dementia,

pass it all on, pass it all away,
that one long message hung out to dry:
'Am in Wolverhampton. Tell Jinny
I'll be back about nine.' Somewhere, someone
wants Aïda, Big Jim Reeves,
news from Serbia and the Cones Hotline

while a cool forest of rain starts
to pack the world with disinformation,
the jumbled code of a Chinese whisper
seeding the air waves
with sound as light, unfocused,
as blood which sang in the ears of the dead . . .

A Victorian Way of Death, 1998

Nearly over, this murmuring and plucking,
shuttering of rooms where in great terror
elders and betters ring for servants
to pound the stairs, fetch coats and sticks,
tickets for somewhere

away from this dull provincial town,
Big C, out in the flatlands. Their indecision
seems to be modelled on the first draft
of Act V in a lost Chekhov.
Grandfather, born in 1852,

with his wall eye, blush-pink fingers,
anecdotes of Paris in the siege,
is comforting grandma, pale and flustered,
dressed in that crushed blue
Ellen never liked much.

A long haul and not what they asked for,
a giant step for two Victorians
whose fingers of brilliants, heavy signet ring
almost touched the twenty-first century.
But here they are dining

in the last chance hospice,
hanging on to it all by a stuttering heartbeat,
a 'Steady, old girl' as the headroom rocks
and their shapes and colours
dim to the storm, go out, go out –

Arras: Easter 1998

Ploughed low the dismissed parade lies
undressed, unmarked. By leaves,
by stems which lean, recover
as the wind sidetracks the grass,
they speak in sighs and exhalations –
two hundred thousand armed men breathing
where shallow draughts of mist
stand easy, and stand to
at first light and when late light dwindles.

For the dead die a little faster this weather,
the skies heavy, water-luminous.
Reflections lie about face-down,
those showers which freshened up
the curls of Chaucer's popinjay from Flanders,
drown memory out, continuous
as the opening Arras barrage
when the shells rode a snowstorm.
Today, the past receives an embassy.

Bearers, kin, and one survivor,
must treat with ghosts at observation posts
of emblazoned stone at Monchy-le-Preux,
by flurrying rain and wind made one
with these 'somtyme in chivachye'
who suffered burial and resurrection
to make some boxfuls of old bones
a theme for yet more spit and polishing:
three Fusiliers, two metal dog-tagged,

late, but uncrimed for this last posting;
their taken names and numbers
restored for eighty years good conduct.
One, obstinate in a dumb insolence,
dispersed his syllables about the earth
and, carried in to this assize, must be
sentenced to the usual reprimand –
'A Soldier of the Great War, Known unto God' –
also to Privates King and Anderson.

Midi

Today and every day Monsieur is dead
but rises from the Famille Mortier
to head this half-laid table of grey sparkles
and dawdle in the purgatory of photograph.
His lip and nose eaten away by light,

his ectoplasmic hair reaching wildly
for the high cirrus where the saints float
their immaculate maculae in iris blue,
he has only a small enthusiasm
for his aquarium of clouded flowers

or the familar similars in his chapped gaze.
In this, our briefest of encounters,
he shows no partiality for Cowper's letters,
or concern for the old Assamese proverb
'To the toothless mouth one slap is hard to bear'

as he waits for night and his poilu sentry-go.
The Stations of the Cross in Sainte Marie
will quiver and jump to violet lightning,
the steeple sharpen up its old 'J'accuse'
through mist-wraiths and mountain-thunders,

but the dead shut up shop these long afternoons,
careless of coarse marguerites, white cattle
dwindling to ghost-selves in the heat-haze,
or the grass sibilant with its long chirpings
of mille regrets, regrets, regrets . . .

Quick-Quick-Slow

They're lightly wondering 'what's become of Joe',
(The Kit-Cat Band, November '26).
Inside that slatted cabinet
Their hottest notes are pleading, yet,
The spiders' legs and flies' wings just don't know.

Cutting her quick-quick-slow from airless air:
my mother's ghost goes into her routine.
The circling dog from HMV
growls dark and gravelly as the sea
and every chord is asking where, oh where

are all those dancers who have danced off-screen,
the Bradford Pals, the shut-eye doll, the cat,
whose *Wanted* posters on the wall
say will-not-come when you-must-call,
however hard you beat the in-between.

But still she makes her diamanté feet
follow the lead of each burnt-out old flame,
tells all the world that it should not
so quite forget what's quite forgot
and shrouded in the wind on dead-end street.

'Gee, but we were happy, not long ago' –
at least we said we were, and that's the same.
For her, for Mary, Theo, Jill,
the jigging hit-squad warbles still
'I wonder what's become of good old Joe.'

Falling Downstairs

Falling downstairs, further, and still falling,
I passed the good dreams hunting for the light,
but the house was black dust in my staring fingers
and the bad dreams tumbled with me into the night
as the raid went head over heels down the snuffed chimneys.

Dragging their sacks of sound into the Midlands,
the Flying Bombs growled over their blazing tails;
I came to grief where the treaders followed the risers
and things were as soft as rot and as hard as nails.
The floor boards walked in their sleep and groaned for
     comfort.

Falling downstairs, further, and still falling,
I bounced the candle-flame off the stinking wick;
the yellow lamp-glass ducked its head in a corner,
the dropped light played its simple vanishing trick
and switched the darkness on like a witch's lantern.

Then the dreams got lost in the dark and punched each
     other,
and the chuckle-headed bombs were having a war,
busy becoming murder and fireside stories.
I hit the bottom rung; love cracked the door
and hauled me through by the hands to the Christmas
     kitchen.

Falling downstairs, further, and still falling,
I clutch at the lost faces, but in my ear
a throat of shining sound is singing for morning,
rubbing it up like Aladdin's lamp: All Clear,
and the sheets frozen to ghosts in an empty bedroom.

Uncle Walt

FOR JOHN MOLE

On the branch-line, coming back,
my head stuck from the carriage,
I watched us duck for the bridge,
in a pother of steam and smoke,

the engine bent on the rails,
by the signal's clack and go.
From all that hullabaloo,
the hot and clinging shawl,

grows a face fringy as cloud,
benign, watery, lost:
the ghost of the family past
who'll never get out of the wood

as he uncouples the carriage
and sets it up at the back
where bluebells fume and smoke,
old sleepers make a bridge

for summer children to go
to where he's gone off the rails
in his potter-about and shawl:
the blue jay's hullabaloo,

the paints which keep getting lost
in a fringy pipe-smoke cloud
as thin as a beech-tree wood,
the slow train signalled past.

A Slice of Cake

I watched her sifting shreds of sun,
with soft and sweet into her bowl.
The air was full of harmless love
which slipped her fingers: lights above,
geraniums with their vixen smell
beyond the glass. The past could say

her hair was trimly tied, tell how
the morning flicked its cleansing tongue
about the room – such lemon zest
for licking scraps. It did its best
to make the knives and glasses ring.
I had my cake, and ate it. Now,

my childhood self, too old to learn
new table-manners, ask for more,
I dare not let him out of sight,
matching my hunger, bite for bite,
a day, a week, a month, a year –
he must have known I would return

for these late crumbs of comfort, wait
for grace, the gift of tongues I lost
between her black and silver hair.
A second slice. We break, we share
as if I still could find the taste
to finish up what's on my plate.

Family Reunion

What can I ask them that I never did,
now that they've walked into this puzzling room
and found me here? Those dialogues of the dead
that litter Landor's pages, lighting time
with wordy lanterns – art, god, politics –
wouldn't quite suit, and, anyhow, they know,
if anyone can know, the river Styx
runs brackish with such baggage. Let it go.
There's still a smell of box, the slanting shades
under the window, and, of course, we'll chat
a bit about the journey. 'Don't be too late
in starting back,' I say – 'the late departed.' 'That,'
my father says, 'is tomfoolery, and you know it –
the sort of remark you'd expect from a minor poet.'

He turns to my books, pulls them out and about
'Not quite all gone to the knacker's yet, I see.'
I know he won't take off his overcoat;
I know she can't stay for a cup of tea.
There must be things to buff and dust below
and kissing-comforts for those awkward neighbours,
some who can name each golden bird and bough,
and picnic-traipses to see Cerberus.
My father, far from home, and restless, hums
'He sold the brick to buy a feather –'
turns briefly to the crossword in The Times
' – and it blew away in the windy weather.'
To say little enough means quite enough has been said.
Why change the habits of a lifetime because you're dead?

Dead right, of course, for when a black hole yawns
'We needn't go into that now' makes perfect sense.
Why mention Cleopatra's nose? What happens,
happens. The rest is of no importance.
I say I'm glad to see them look so well,
and he 'The change has done wonders for Dorothy.'
It seems a good idea to keep the talk small,
defer, as usual, to their assumed maturity.
They look as if they've chosen how to look,
deep in the prime of a late middle-age –
work to be done, but time for gardens, walks,
gadding off on some petty pilgrimage.
'Peter's books are so much neater than yours were, John.'
'That's because he never reads them.' Chit-chat goes on

as if I'd written it myself. And God?
'An agreeable enough little man,' he says –
his clinch on parleys with the great and good.
'You look yourself more like the Ancient of Days
with hair like that – or the Wild Man of Borneo.'
In this sub-Yeatsian trembling of the veil,
there seems some little distance left to go
before I can divine the immanent will.
Angels? I hazard. 'Optional, if you're C. of E.
Dorothy, look at that ridiculous cat.'
And she? 'I'm a Christian, except for immortality
and the soul. I don"t believe in all that.'
As a cloud gathers, no bigger than a man's hand,
I ask her what other excursions they've got planned.

'We're on our way to visit Mother.' Yes,
but who on earth is 'Mother' going to see?
They'll have to change between the acts, confess
grey hairs and wrinkled skin pure mummery;
How are they wanted? Decked in sailor-suits,
a tea-gown, Oxford bags, a little fur
with shining paws . . . ? I have no doubts,
their dress-codes being what they always were –
'You can't come with me till you've brushed your hair' –
that they can pull such wools across the eyes
as the occasions call for. 'It's not far,'
she says, but this is where he mutinies:
'My dear good woman . . .' he starts. Dumbed by déjà-vu,
I feel it's a blessing they're only passing through,

for clearly, there's not much they want to know
except that rose's name, whether the pond
has newts, what I am teaching – time hangs slow
upon the clock. Why lend a helping hand
to my intrusive jigsaw stuffed with holes
whose bits they've always hidden, screwed up tight
in tears and silences, or old wives' tales
of Billy Brumpton, Theo, kissing-gate
or college-court. Then, his defensive quote:
'Deep questioning, that probes to endless dole . . .
I think we should leave the touchy-feely bit
to Doubting Thomas.' That old recoil.
Smiling, they turn – are gone. No handshake, kiss for mother;
it's much too late now for seeing through each other.

Parting

'Parting?' Yes, to die, and more than a little:
carry the poetry peculiar to that word
from banks and shores of sunlight –
the shining stuff you thought no slick could foul –
past cloud-hems into – something.

For this bed – sweat-stains,
linens falling to the cold sea-floor –
was always what the sunlight led to.
You played in childhood at being dead
and look, it all came true,

learning to hold your breath for ever,
the bed singling itself out
to a drunk boat, a one-man crew
slipping anchor from these ivory coasts
to trawl in depths of ebony,

where, hopelessly in love with shadows,
you racked yourself to the mast
against their strong seductions,
knowing those dead reaches; the dead reaching
across and into you for landfall.

Crossing the Peak

Crossing the Peak, unsingled stars
broke from cloud, hung on the lines
which drew them into gods and heroes.
Saw, low in its laval cauldron,

Manchester threshed to amber,
trapped in shrouds of earth-light:
each voice, each singular, abrupt,
incorrigible voice quite lost.

What broke loose then, could not.
The car-roof was drummed stupid.
Some huge entanglement of wing,
some claw, racked and pinioned,

skating its hooks on cold metal.
Had night stooped to kill,
brought a Fury out of hiding
to ride my shames bareback?

The hours removed themselves
into a deep vow of silence.
West became East again.
North grew to South, slowly.

The Northern Line

END OF LEAVE, 1950S

I   BOARDING

Kit in first, I wave to trees and no one,
then take huge gulps of smoke and chill,
my head slung from the window's shoulders.
Things creak and sniff, start monkey-chattering
through low-flying cloud and belts of rain;
metal floors part and greet themselves,
thick up with dog-ends; doors hang about
over piss-pools, trampled paper.
Two fish-cold sleepers, mouths agape,
float in unrinsed light. In Ashwell church
our foolish tribulations are incised in stone:
'A great wind blows through the world,
and only the dregs of the people left.'
Night grows luminous with false perceptions
and up in his yellow cage the signalman
is a silhouette whose arms are strong enough
to haul his lever through a change of tenses,
switch the points the whole shebang must head for.
Night pothers out a film of greasy stars
over chalked-up trucks, the Dickens thing
of big wheels, stovepipe hats and chimneys,
trains 'gliding on like vast weird funerals'
through burning meat-smells in the Welwyn tunnels,
and 'unknown languages in the air, conspiring
in red, green and white characters'.
My shoulder strap cossets my beret, badged
Sua Tela Tonanti – to the thunderer his weapons.

Some delight, to grin like a gormless thing,
sway, drunk on a fierce night-wind,
skelter down a swung flare-path,
locked in the banshee wail, Joe Miller's jest-book
riddling away at nothing, nothing at all.
'Why is a chicken when it spins?'
'Because one of its legs is both the same.'
The knives flicker, paring back
to the core, the stalk, the longed-for absence.
Khaki rubs at the neck's nape;
the badge catches at light: *Sua Tela Tonanti*,
and a crown which crowns a million skulls.
Under Vimy Ridge mines packed and primed
sap out their Ammonal. In the lit city,
patched by criss-cross feet, scar-tissue,
dark-finned bombs wait with uncrazed skins
who followed their noses into the Roman dark:
bones, oyster-shells, sandal-thongs, brickbats,
shadowy centurions, masons of Mithras,
driving ghosts hard who still can't tell
their sinister from their dextra.
Tucked in far silos, clean-cut missiles doze
under strong enchantments of code and key.
Who will cosset them into nightmare,
help them sing like stars in the glory
of their imperium? I brace myself
against the pull of England, on the curve.

3   JUNCTION

Hanamanoosh, hanamanoosh,
all the sixes, clickety-click. Wheels
pound at the cracks, the discontinuities
in these long tricks of shine that tell the night
'Follow the gleam, follow the gleam'
to where the signal's clip-clop stiffens
us into drag, a stuttered run-down,
a dull slide by shelves of puddled concrete.
Jolts. The slam of doors. Then nothing.
Only a voice, garbled and rough as God,
denouncing the stations of the cross.
'The steam hissed. Someone cleared his throat.
No one left and no one came' –
except the usual suspects of the time
who drift up in a press of awkward shadows.
How much will each compartment hold:
sixteen moustached poilus, eight horses
cut loose from Mark Gertler's roundabout?
Eccles, Bluebottle and Moriarty
double up under a gigantic doll,
its sallow face cowlicked, toothbrush-tached,
its right and awkward arm saluting nothing.
Anna Neagle, a Cameron Highlander,
head matchstuck on with Harbutt's plasticine,
a corpse-white milkman with a leaden face
balancing his pails like scales of justice –
Then, the long whistle with its sexless thrill.

Doctor and Housewife have done their duty,
turned blind eyes to love's refreshment room,
its white orphanage of cups and saucers
as cold as charity or a shut sunday,
as hoped-for, never-to-be-given kisses. Now
the Guard's flag flicks green for danger
and whoomph, whoomph go thick smoke-beats
as faceless dream-girls wave their hankies,
Gothic windows blub and snivel,
strung lights coagulate. The Stationmaster
raises his baton and the band strikes up:
'Oh we don't want to lose you,
but we think you ought to go . . .'
What a send-off for the cold war captains
high-staking it in a first-class compartment,
tobacco-wreaths drifting sagacity
about the forehead of each fellow-traveller:
Dulles and Eisenhower play Brinkmanship;
Stalin and Molotov, at Stakes and Leaders,
wash undigested countries down with vodka,
growl of executions, wolves and medals.
Churchill – 'the voice that breathed o'er Eden' –
slumps balefully while his marionette
languidly picks my number from his Homburg,
despatches me to Suez – where I will not go.
'Never mind what they all say, my dear,
but take a return ticket every time the train stops.'

Back, back to the land of the midnight sun,
the Hornby loco set for Rockery Junction
and long derailments under the elder
which still holds out its musty memory-clusters
over bright, battered liveries of war,
scattered among marigolds and shrapnel.
Back to the keys which wound the past too tight,
the fizz of clockwork, and the broken spring.
Back to the branch-line, Snelland, Wickenby,
the tired old brutes that clanked and puffed
before the Reverend Awdry got at them,
the sentiment of bells, clock-faces, milk churns,
a lattice of sweet-peas blown by light
into a summer coronation.
Back to a melancholia of shut wagons
shunting the bombers' night into the sidings
with a long, sonorous diminuendo.
Back to the Gatehouse.
                    Later, came to a different conclusion.
The smell of steam is for ever the smell of dying.
After that 'first powerful, plain manifesto
The black statement of pistons'— what?
The lament of the birches at Birkenau,
and half a century's epitaph: *Arbeit Macht Frei.*
Back to Derby station, father hunting corpses
under the arc-lights and the rubble smell.
To the thunderer his weapons.

The wheels spin backwards, and the train
lurches to terminus. Unstud the window strap,
Let it kick back into the door frame.
Hit the ground running. The engine blows its top.
'Soldier, I'll have you off this square so fast
your feet won't touch the ground' –
the Underground. I float past sleepers
wrapped in their shrouds, government issue,
Henry Moore, Mark One. In my kit,
Baudelaire, the London Book of English Verse,
sing lightly to the unborn dead
who will not turn their heads to look at me,
trapped in the invisible cloak of uniform
like Chesterton's postman. Somehow –
Farewell, Leicester Square – I must meet
my Waterloo, thread this place of changes
where my hair tingles with prognostication.
A busker flower-powers his guitar –
'Where have all the soldiers gone,
gone to graveyards every one' –
and City gents hurry to strap-hang home
from The Blitz Experience, The London Dungeon,
neatly funereal under Magritte faces.
Celia Johnson, eyes bunged up with tears
hurries past the gangling man with dreadlocks,
and push-me pull-you trains with moony faces
cry 'Follow, follow, follow me'.

'Shun the frumious Bandersnatch'
doped to the eyeballs, unexploded luggage,
the moving staircase, and the sliding door.
'Up and down this world goes round, down.'
Mind the gap. For this, our travelling grave,
the vacuum makes its little sigh of closure,
the Northern Line parts to speed our passing.
No conversations. Only, off the rails,
the scream of Orpheus in the Underground
'A bodiless childfull of life in the gloom,
crying with frog voice, What shall I be?'
I am 22651134, the toybox soldier
twenty-two million, six hundred and fifty-one
thousand, one hundred and thirty-three later
than Private Cain, MM, the oldest sweat of all
who eats the ones like me for breakfast.
I have punched my number into my mess-tin.
It must be true. Here is my hand to prove it.
Someone up in the sky is fond of numbers,
knows how many flying miles and inches
I travel daily from the place called home.
This catacomb grows slippery with skulls
beaten from light, 'Follow the gleam.'
Strip off our foolish clothes, this metal shell-case,
laugh to see us burrowing mother-naked,
bent for sitting, standing with one arm raised
in hope of resurrection, and the life to come.

Raising their fish-cold faces to the light,
their mouths agape for stony crumbs of comfort
from the Evening Standard – Late Night Extra,
the Chronicles and Heralds of stale beer,
the nudes descended must ascend the staircase.
We gaze tremulously at the family portraits
of girls in Berlei bras, gents in Aquascutums
and smarten up those glad-rags handed in
to giant rats in the Quartermaster's Stores,
or given to the daily help, or Oxfam.
I carry myself as luggage to the concourse
and here I am, in *camino del mezzanine*,
feeling a bit shaky, a touch of flu
or of the golden birds, watching what's past
or passing, or, in these glasses dimly,
what's to come. *Sua Tela Tonanti.*
I pat my beret, sharpen up my pleats –
'His smart bearing and efficient manner
have made him an asset to his unit.'
Back to Basic Training, civvies parcelled home,
perhaps from Escort Duty, Embarkation Leave;
who never got to Cyprus, Egypt, Cythera
glimpsed Naafi nautch-girls throwing flowers
and singing love-songs to the westering moon,
the calme, the luxe, the whole volupté bit.
Time enough, though, for a lipstuck cup of tea
with Baudelaire and his red-haired beggar-girl.

'C'est magnifique, mais ce n'est pas la gare' –
Somebody has turned the volume down,
halted the goose-step of my second-hand,
stopped those digits racing into nowhere.
I think of a week in the Collège Stanislaus
on the Boul' Mich, lectures at the Sorbonne –
Servitude et Grandeur Militaires –
a kiss under the Pont Neuf, strikes on the Metro,
home with my 78's, Claude Luter, Sidney Bechet.
Scribbling in pencil under yellow light,
I lose the poetry in my translation:
'Those begging arms should only pray
some other to your charms' display . . . '
I'm conscious of that bent, oldish man who looks
as if he'd like to catch my eye. He's *there*
as the first star you cannot see by staring.
'*À une Mendiante Rousse.* What did our father say –
Beware loose girls – you should be so lucky!
The next line you want will go like this –
'and chase his teasing hands away'.
You look dubious? Yes, I was, too.
It's very possible 'we'll meet again,
don't know where, don't know when'.
Hang on to that anthology, that Baudelaire
I've lent you. I'll expect to see them
back on my shelves when I get home.
Goodbye. 'You, that way; we, this way'.

Stunned, I write the line down without thinking,
watch him weave the concourse, dodge
three German girls with rucksacks, push past
this carnival that's going wildly on,
the stripy candyhats filling baguettes,
the Military Police, the chinless wonders
fresh with their Mons or Eaton Hall commissions.
And as for me, stuff's waiting down the line:
a Pompey Coronation Fleet that's all lit up,
more juvenilia torn for their bad verses –
'The soldiers stamp about the square,
Defaulters wait by Majors' Dens,
The dirty offices are filled
With the sad scratch of pay clerks' pens' –
and long night-strolls putting the 'fifties right
with Corporal David Winnick, MP.
Old queens, false knights, young rookies,
and Elvis Presley yowling *Muss i' denn.*
That's all to come. There's my train.
It fills up with the dead, the real soldiers
from Neuve Chapelle, Dunkirk or the Ardennes,
who take up all the room there is and none,
their pallid kit-bags stencilled fiercely
Tommy Atkins, Nobby Clark, Dusty Miller . . .
back to their squares, the Indian verandahs,
and waxed moustaches of their Sergeant-Majors.
Sua Tela Tonanti. I face the engine's music
in a black Pacific at the tag-end of steam.

'And then there came both mist and snow.'
Up there. Cape Wrath. Ultima Thule.
At Carlisle, below the stumbled wall,
Paul Nash paints a new Totes Meer:
Northern lines, where the dead ride at anchor
and all our loves and partings come to this –
the disjecta membra of clack box, frame stay,
bogie guard and steam chest cover,
whistles handle, sight-feed lubricator –
poor tarnished ivories of the graveyard.
To the thunderer his weapons.
Here, at the crossroads of a century,
arc-welders flense each carcass.
In masks and fountains of white fire,
pull down the Castles, Kings and Cities
into the raw materials of desire.
'Attendant, with many a clank and wrench,
were lumbering cares, dark meditations,
huge dim disappointments, monotonous years.'
Troubles packed up in the old kit-bags
have drifted out through rusty eyelets
and cannot find their ghostly comforters;
the chilled air is blown about with kisses,
dries on the cheek like an unwiped tear-stain,
like rain, drying. 'Thus, at Mugby Junction,
at past three o'clock of a tempestuous morning,
the traveller went where the weather drove him.'

Night Watch

The branch rocks the moon off, on;
animal heat springs out a flare
on steps, concrete, the ribby glass
in the vehicle park. It won't go far,

as light goes, but each bit helps,
as the glimpse of a named thing or star
helps. For heat after blood and treasure,
it's a cold, small day up there,

and squarely cornered by night.
The girl stretched on the calendar
wears out her skin's uniform
slowly, slowly. A chair

squawks. Helmets in Trônes Wood
are holed by rust. Every door
is a question for this bunch of keys
whose wards fail to answer

that slow pulse on the stair,
the pushed-about dust. Easier
to lie unclutched on the table,
look gleamily up at her

as she moves to answer his heat,
short-change their silver,
open herself to the tree, the dark
in blackface and balaclava.

Night Kitchen

Headlamps glancing away from night ahead
glaze the room over, pausing for a moment
in the sheen and hopeful dust which flows from,
sticks to, the pretty cups and their sadness.
Whatever is being searched for, hunted down,
darkness will not be taken for an answer.

Everything which happens happens in passing.
The kitchen drowses in light, that nervous stranger
coasting lost into a place of secrets.
Things here have made love to each other so often,
undressing each other's colours nightly,
that his embarrassment is hardly noticed

as the chair sleeps in the clock's arms,
what has been left out finds itself really in bed,
the cats and spoons grow desolate and cosy.
At the window, a spectral twirl of roses,
and, in the room, something being raised –
which could be yesterday, that ghost of a smile

haunting the lazy plates which will not finish
themselves up, or get down from the table
for this visitor playing at seeing how long
he can hold his pale breath over, under, water;
whose brief composure is carelessly ruffled
by the sink-tap, crying slowly in blobs of sound

which nobody wants to hear. It is all on offer;
appearances cannot be saved. The films unreel
in a flurry of nothing, the fingerprints drift
away from each surface into the hands of a stranger
who paces himself through the dark, his eyes
bent on away, white gloves calming the wheel.

In the Picture

A heavy man holds a frame about his head,
twirling it round in a slow dance while the city
goes about its business of the movements
of its dull clock with no escapement

fractioned in turn, passed glimmeringly on.
There's not really much to choose
between this and great lancets meshed with iron.
The glazier's art specifies nothing but seasons,

that spidery wait for an eye which might appraise
each minute boredom of blue, each belly
of slow-breeding cloud. You could hope
for something more than people, birds or stars

as a heavy man makes a tedious film,
and out of this window the packed greens
in my field of vision wobble with light.
Quickening air takes their converse apart

while Mr and Mrs Andrews wait by a cornfield;
the world's skylights lie flat on their backs
with extraordinary views of nothing at all
reaching its ceiling. The clouds dissolve

and a smudged view stares at the back of a man
framed by a city room, watching a film
of his own slow, insufferable dance:
a heavy man, twirling yesterday's business.

Nothing at All

Nothing at all out there today but a name
that could be 'mist', which is before one's eyes,
or 'fog': too active, swirling about in its chapter,
though the tumbledown house is pushy enough,
riding its angles into the heart of whiteness

as if close-hauled, its wormy timbers braced
against the shock of some darker, whiter hulk
steering itself, steered or anchored
in the over-there drenched and sodden stuff;
fuming or steaming away into that name

which must be 'mist', but not 'love-in-a-mist',
not today, though that is love's habitat,
unless to wait, and see without watching
how a bare chart, a sky which cannot be compassed,
tempt definition, are, possibly, love,

and 'love' is a word, hoping also for definition,
as on the edge, approaching the curfew of mist
is a line of trees, their sprits bare of canvas,
a clean palisade of leaf-pointed, vertical iron,
and beyond, just beyond, those metres of rough

something: dead ground or slack water,
receding, filling, promising nothing at all
but a hardness to hurt, a depth to drown in,
as what can be seen moves out to meet its conclusion
where the bell's clapper is tied, and Cordelia silent.

A Trunk of Letters

Is this the chapter where the treasure-seekers,
flinging the lid back, rinse their hands in gold?
Listen – the gulls. The sky breaks up their voices.
which might have consequential things to say
about snapped wish-bones and a sandy bay,
the cave's ribbed window, attic salt, and cold –

but no, the dropped scraps of such conversations
run out into the bladderwrack and foam.
This sea-chest disappoints: all cling-film faces
and little creepings underneath the skin,
brittle green ribbons and a black-head pin,
a night of family faces coming home

to roost, to babble volumes in, confess
how much they missed each other, what they read
in faces that were not yet photographs.
Their news, as common as the common cold,
as flowers or visits, work, or growing old,
grows rare and nervous just by being dead,

as cursive, itching fingers whisper on
'We mapped this land, charted the deep-sea swell,
and time and tide were in our reckoning.
Not now, not you. See how our crosses mark
heart-burials.' In the November dark
the shaken house keens like a giant shell.

In Camera

They swim in and out of focus, the Campo Santo's
depth of field, the stone exposures of time
in the postcards you bought, and sent abroad,
which was home, to lie for their country,
the snaps you took yourself in the Mezzo del Camin:
those greens, reds, indigos, that little museum
with a wall-eyed dog and paintings by Circa,
the cobbled alley which led you down and on
past boys pirouetting on bikes to a view of the sea

where clouds which are far too white blow over
the lacklustre names of poets and senators.
Today, somebody else, wearing your camera,
takes a picture of difference, and calls it beauty,
though beauty is nothing much to write home about,
especially that view of the sea, chop-chopping away
at a headland stiff with confectionery houses,
trim, childish trees and a church whose gloom
is primped by time-shares in everlasting candles.

In this place your affections must make-believe in,
stay-at-homes shoot lines for the traveller
wild as the musketry of their cherished insurrection,
and haunting the junk-shop window a curling postcard.
shows your mother and father crossing the street
by a huge parked car with white-walled tyres.
They are looking away from the sun-blanked square,
with its flags, shoulder-straps and floral lamp-posts
for a last view of the sea on the way to the station,

three trains and a difficult channel-crossing.
She is thinking of you; he is thinking of Arnold –
the *Scholar Gipsy* – and how much to leave in tips.
It is there in black and white. On scraps of pasteboard
dying in cupboards lurk views full of faces –
the lovers, the banker, the man selling bread –
nobody posed for, no one will ever identify
while the photographer, intent on a somewhere
watches for sunlight to sharpen his view of the sea

and all the forgettable people go briskly on,
or pause while a match is struck, a glance taken
at something mildly important, and, like the dodo,
dead. Is it you, there, propped in the shadow,
aiming your poem into the sunlight, under the notice
'Please do not shoot the photographer – he is only
doing his best?' For you, your parents, a view of the sea,
two cake-walking sentries outside the Palais de Justice,
the marsupials pouched in the zoological gardens

must be drawn deep, deeper, more deeply yet
into that swell of glass whose fanciful tremblings
of light mirror those on that view of the sea
framed in a Kodak entre deux guerres,
with its bob of girls in stripes and bathing-caps
growing ever more hungry for metempsychosis,
where click, each fluttering thing – *animula vagula blandula* –
must lose its name, become small, flat, so very still,
yet born again, having seen the light, and been saved.

The Old Home

It is Happy Hour in the Cavalier Hotel.
Executives bark and clink at the Long Bar,
laughing the dusk down into its wishing-well.
While Harold fetches the bags in from the car
Doris looks at the window-catch. From where she is sitting
its bobble brass-hat looks back like French knitting.

And she thinks 'Is it happy?', watches Mary come through
to make up the fire, collect the tea-things.
Such stuff in her head making such a to-do.
There's Dads and Mr Errold by the till, confabulating,
as Harold used to say, about Tuesday's auction
and how something must be done about old Mrs Jackson.

And are they happy? The ghost of a tennis-ball
slams into the car-park over half-standard roses.
Behind the door marked 'Dames' in the Long Bar wall
a convulsion of water. The Doulton font
disposes of things. The flush-pull, that porcelain
cold as a skull. Is it happy, does it complain?

And Dads is saying 'She never says much, our Doris',
while Mr Errold walks right through her table, slow,
wheezing a little, trimming the yellow gas,
as if there was a little light it could throw
on Death by Chocolate, Rombout's coffee, Pevsner,
the fairy packets of low-calorie sweetener

which might make things happy. Harold looks like trouble.
'I'd best see to the room.' Upstairs, in Number 4,
Alice must be sitting with a Gideon Bible.
She has sleepy sickness. Everyone has a cross to bear.
Dads is tugging at the catch, the dratted thing,
which needs mending, and mends nothing.

Lunch Out

is sitting on grass, hardish, with dogs.
Most do nothing ever so slowly,
unleashed for an hour in their odd cool hats,
dazed out. Jazz clears its throat, sun
buffs the works up in silver and gold,
boats

Clamber about in the cut. Ground,
somewhat downtrodden, perks up enough
for a colourable view of enormous legs,
swatches of bosom and buttock
becalmed over canvas, riding a stiff
sargasso

which will not pull to their foundering
old age with a hatful of ribbons,
the blue man trapped in his tuba,
the singer who sings his invisible toes
to the sunny side of the street,
the girl

strutting again with some barbecue
through children, hatchings of shade,
the processional rise and fall
of glasses always half-full, never half-empty.
Two ancient girls promenade, sashay,
parasols

dipped to the wind off the horn, twirled
in a flutter of gaudy. Out there
soundless and congruent triangles
part the water, as if to be white and happy
were in itself an excuse for not being
dead.

The Letter

I

Twin curtains, trussed against outside,
and stiff as Tudor grave-clothes with ruched topknots:
the room's in hibernation, closed on its fog-smell,
a dead-spice cabinet dreaming of quickened voices,
but only the clock lives for the moments

which rock themselves to sleep in cradles of dust.
A swollen light-bulb with its airy keening
pores over boxes, gives a cluttered table
the spit and polish of pure definition,
picks up a letter you could almost see through,

while stone-washed linen holds an unused day,
glass, following its water-course,
ripples, thickens at the pane's foot.
Something holds its breath; the weeping eye
brightens a little, darkens a little,

as the room starts up and stops. A mirror
plays back the fluster of these tips and wrinkles:
those throbbing filaments, that dying nerve
which sings its tiny love-song to the dark,
and though it tricks with habits of command,

knows that its spell of opening must fail
to stir this clouded concourse: doors and curtains
closed in the compass of a walnut-shell.
Now, only the hands of time, grown luminous,
the unanswered letter, asking to be addressed.

II

The clock, scribbling in longhand, shorthand,
never finds time to reconsider its message.
but says it all in a chattering class of wheels
and a cold heart sleeved under a bell-jar.
Dirt plays with dirt, is written off and away.
For keeps. There's a long chain-letter somewhere,
and only one promise made. Nobody reads it;

the promise will keep till kept. More news
throws its light on nothing heading for nowhere:
the cat sicks up, a rose fingers the window,
there's a fall of soot. It is the clock's office
to note these little deaths, and unrecord them.
Roman hours grow quainter by the minute;
feathers drift into the Grand Canyon

and someone comes into the room: a shadow,
a frown crossing the air, as if in this puzzle
something might be put straight, the bulb changed,
curtains drawn, dead flowers wreathed
in a basket of currency no longer current.
The clock pretends it has stopped. In silence,
the byway of sound, a hand looks for the letter.

It is there, where you dropped it. The words
float off the page, as eyes get used
to the passage of time. A marquetry box
dissolves its inlay into a cluster of shades;
they worry themselves to the back of beyond,

the clock comes apart in its hands,
and breaks a shower of meteors over a table
tipping and sliding away as the spirit moves it.
There is only the letter, ready to unfold
its questioning answers: 'Dear one,

You ask for news? Well, I must chronicle
such small beer as our life is made of.
Pascal's been sick again. It comes
of eating mouse on a full stomach. The Albertine
needs pruning – we can hardly see into the garden.

You can't imagine the mess the room's in.
A bird must have got caught in the chimney.
Soot everywhere . . .' Things grow garrulous.
A pinch of air sniffs at the curtains,
locks the sunlight up in a field of glass

where the rose wanders, and goes still.
The clock looks for the time; clicking its teeth,
finds it. On the letter primed with invisible ink,
a responsive hand draws words into a circle
as up on the high wire, light sings to the dark.

Trevail: Four Children & Summer

A little further. Now you have put yourself
in the picture, look at the children
as they prop out flat on a huge boulder,
facing the space you have walked away from.
Feel their flesh, slabbed cold and wet
and red with the impress of ground-up shell.
There is noise in the air, that familiar blend
of gulls with childhood's animal cry,
a ribboned pleasure-boat snoring into the wind.
There is a place here for you, but no welcome

from those four faces: only a mobile sea
tearing off strips of itself to lay on the sand.
Walk past them – you might try
to find the towels, the cooling thermos,
the camera, safely lost in your empty hands,
the paperback in the raffia basket
whose words have washed quite through,
and possibly over, your head,
Call to them. The words die in your throat
as if, sleep-sticky, you called to wake them,

and yourself, from the drops and edges of things,
to cry with the voice of the wind
an alarm for each fizzing cauldron,
each hole where the Atlantic slams its door
on the dark, or salutes the dying of time
with a dull processional gun. It's late,
so trudge back to the unturned heads,
salt-licked skin, still and quivering limbs,
and, as you pass them, pick them up, and watch
the sun strike home against their unblinking eyes.

Kippford: A View from the Bridge

The transparency
of a transparency:
the sky that day
something borrowed,
something blue.

Three on a plank bridge,
brothers and sister,
sprawl over water:
the slight burn brackish
and moving slowly,

their whispering hair
with its bleached look
spread like twitch
the wind rubs down
in the Traffords' field.

The projector's fan
winnows light;
with a soft whirr:
something winged
might take its flight

to hover, sing,
over the children's
view from a bridge,
where ageing faces
rise to greet them.

Lea Valley: My Son, My Father

Half-deep in flowers, not thinking of time
as it quietly thinks of them, they are, it seems,
two of the happiest prisoners of summer,
closed in greens and blues and the forest of names
it is second nature for the older one to know.
Nothing is happening. Nothing is likely to happen.
Somebody must have said that morning
'Shall we go to . . . ?' So, a little fuss, and here they are.
Parked by this photo, its bonnet juggling the air,
a neat car fills with heat, the road-map lies open,
a cluster of sweets joins hands in the glove compartment.

She rests the camera, walks into the wood,
and leaves this day which is hard to forget, or remember –
an insistent pleat of light in the family album.
The two of them stand easily, and to attention
under a pile of yesterday's papers and knitting
shifting its weight over thickets of grass
which do not droop, but fill the room with a dry
fragrance plucked from damp and darkness.
They look to the cleft of a stream, lost at their feet,
their ears tripped on its clean runnels of sound
while the keys to it all hang dead still from the fascia.

Epithalamion

FOR ROGER SCUPHAM AND JENNIFER CASSELS

New foliage grows to a head on familial trees,
and a thousand hieroglyphs cut by time's leaf-borers
print out their message for the millennial wind.
Though the air grows cold with prognostication,
somewhere, someone is picking a leaf, and reading
'I love you', however runic the language.

Thunder and lightning bounce below the horizon.
Under that ledge of cloud or nightfall, the Schwarzwald
lurks on the marches of the Märchen; there misfortunes
weave thickets of bat-skin, huts grow dark with cloaks
pledged by ogres and witches who curse nightly,
but cannot say 'I love you' in any language,

and are put to flight by the simplest of white magics,
a ring danced on a finger, an exchange of glances.
Let harpies harp away on their one-string fiddles;
in your sunlit Cirque d'Hiver, as the black and white horses
step out in their keyboard tandem, let music say
'I love you' in a language which pays no duty,

and, unpoliced by savage hats and holsters,
is at home in a polis whose frontiers are always open,
whose sunlight mints to silver those flyaway wings
which stitch the Old World and the New together,
and whispers down snow-cold slopes of air
a constant green-world promise to earth: 'I love you,

your trees which dance, die, dance: andante, allegro,
which tell each other that something is always for ever,
though branches thrust and fall, the clung mould thickens.'
What can the green leaves say in the face of winter,
except that, however dead the language, the words
'I love you' are never lost in the new translation.

Song for Sophie

A GRANDDAUGHTER, BORN 1998

The world is full of wishes
that sparkle up in fountains,
ride the blackest cats.
They steal a flock of crosses
and blow them into kisses,
pull flowers out of mountains,
rabbits out of hats.

On a far-off yesterday
the first wish hid in darkness
till someone wished it true,
wished lions, cars and postmen,
daisies, mice and milkmen,
and liking all that likeness,
wished, of course, for you.

When you read these verses,
guess by words and spaces
what their wish might be,
thinking hard of postmen
daisies, mice and milkmen –
packed tight with wishes
and saying just like me

each is special, singular,
together in their dancing,
in out, up down, sun, moon, star.
In a packet or a pocket
keep your wish a secret
and tell it just by being
exactly who you are.

The Christmas Owl

I

Christmas Eve: the lilt,
the syllable. Ice
puckers the roadside:
snow on the wind.
The cats will not talk tonight
but weather dances
on the point of a needle
which sets north-east.
Let it sleep if it will
the house in the village
with its riding-lights
bobbing the air-waves,
the tumbril of beet
at the field's groyne.
Let it all sleep:
robes cling like bats
in the vestry cupboard,
Donner and Blitzen
sledge through nowhere.
What can unwrap
the ribboned room?

II

Bees do not sing
in their crowded hive,
no cocks crow
to the numb moon,
but somebody shakes
four hundred years
down the chimney flue:
a Lord of Misrule
with doll-glass eyes
and a wand of wings
to cut and shuffle
the cooling air.
A house of cards
flakes from the mantel;
in high bat-voice
a nest of baubles
chinks from the tree.
Its plump doublet
basted with soot,
Strix Aluco,
the Tawny Owl.

III

Christmas Day.
No shepherds cried
'Ut hoy, ut hoy.'
Nipped blood, foul ways,
we sit like mice
in a dim tree-house
whose hollow trunk
breathes out our breath,
sleepy-eyed
for a little pitcher
with hidden ears.
Whatever is born
to this clouded light
must come to the hooks
beneath the plush.
The murderers too
will need such patience:
wings locked on
and seeking heat
from more than cold
that cuts to the bone.

Riches Heures du Duc de Berry

Seeing, but mostly through, past filmy blueness
patching at star-creep up against the window,
past leaves and branches blotted on free evenings
which rocked the house-glow in their oily cradles,
you looked for something that might be a token.
When all they said was 'Seeing is believing',
what then was seeing but a loose lantern
swung in the night, blindly-starred, and waiting
for light to clean its gates of horn and ivory,
then jump through tiny hoops cut in blue paper
on bedroom darkness rising like a fountain.

The choirstall mullions were infilled by stars
pinned over saints in blood and emerald,
and fierce in judgement when the sun came out
suspended by a press of waxen clouds.
A saint should have stars fountained over him,
a jovial shower of light for each dull nimbus.
Chained at my wrist, a moon-face watch recycles
one simple blue, a splutter of gold ink
as childish, jostled out of constellation,
as the night-sky on my sudden screen-save
or heaven daubed about a wizard's cloak.

Calendar pages, where the so-rich hours,
those cloaks betrothed to blues and silences,
lie weightless to the grass as Disney towers
lie weightless to the hill, your pale, jimp faces
are not inclined to hear our conversations,

but turn to where the sky-beasts penned in azure
perch level-headed among equal stars
dancing a touch, grown fey and tremulous
as coins which have learned to live in fountains:
clusters of spent wishes wished by some
too young or old for seeing and believing.

Kilvert's Winter: 1871

I

Light lords it over Draycot Water,
a whole chinoiserie of lanterns
papering over fire in blue, green, crimson.
They keep delightful station
as Harriet Awdry jumps over a punt,
Arthur Law jumps over a chair,
the cow jumps over the moon
and all the magnesium ribands cry 'Bravo!'
to fire boxed in a roaring pen at the lakeside.
The ice is in splendid order,

sliders and slitherers roped away
from the fancy dancers, heirs and Graces,
the Sydneys, Pagets, Roystons,
and a Mr Calcroft they call 'The Hangman'.
To the strains of a quadrille band
the starlight dances the Lancers,
Snow falls. Men beat the bounds.
To a whisk of brooms, the Gentry
cut their finest figures,
wheel in a circuit of torches.

II

In a room pungent with lime chloride.
Maria Kilvert, a white sheet drawn over,
lies lapped in lead, lapped in oak
lined with white satin.
Authority melts from the face
frozen down into silence.
He steals a silver seal.

On Christmas Day, such cold:
brush and sponge stiff and stark.
Breaking the sheet-ice,
he bathes in broken chandeliers,
his loins jousting with sherds,
cries hosannna through the burning,
the split prisms, the bells.

Mary Price stares at an angel
perched on her arm in grave-clothes
and a child's coffin-cap.
Young Meredith's jaw is locked.
They wrench it open with a screw,
can do nothing for him.
Catherine's skin falls away like scurf.

A thinnish crowd skates at Draycot:
such antics from a German lady's maid
as you would expect. Lord Royston sulks.
'Those abominable Miss Awdrys
have contradicted me about the Lancers.'
Lord Cowley, struck by a fiery torch
bangs it about, roaring in fury,
Mr Calcroft takes a heavy tumble.
'Where did you lie last, Hangman?'
A little laughter shines in the bushes.

Tonight there are children calling,
their voices everywhere, so many,
and men are out beating the holly,
beating for blackbirds with a clap-net.
On the Bowood ice, Mr Greenwood's son,
breaks his head on a stone,
dies in an hour by the lakeside.
Children call from the hills
in a great frost and a cloudless sky.
They must be sliding on moonlight.

The Chairs

'She takes away the confidence one should have in her chair
if she were once out of it.' – DR JOHNSON

Beat that, poor mouse.
There's so much brilliance going on it hurts.
'Pray, sir, let me help you to another slice of wisdom,
but none of your sauce.' How can silence,
which, as he knows, propagates itself,
be refuted, except by kicking it
and setting the poor bruised table on a roar.

In drab, in mouse,
no heart to heave her heart into her mouth,
no spark to fan with lesser lights and lustres
who congregate about this luminary,
she'd blush to find herself in his concordance,
her table place reserved
to feed the grossness of his humour.

And there she sits,
her chair drawn up into that conversation
where Coleridge rabbits on to someone's button,
Goethe chats up a stone, hedge-philosophers
apostrophise the trees they cannot see
for woods that they are lost in.
A chair is true enlightenment,

feet on the ground
four-square, at ease, taking a social polish,
perfectly in control of legs and arms.
'I say a chair has a bottom of good sense.
A chair is fundamentally sensible.'

It can accommodate John Wilkes
without embracing Whiggish notions

and will absorb
the long weariness of cumbered flesh,
a mind unsettled by the Bench, the Woolsack.
'No more of that, sir!' His veins throb,
and Lady Macdonald lurks in the Hebrides,
mouth open, hands propping her cheeks:
'insipidity on a monument',

as growling, ticking,
he swims against a tide of well-bred faces
to take tea-chat with dead, neglected Tetty,
be alone for just one evening with Molly Aston,
'not happiness, but rapture'.
How they would talk their chairs invisible,
quite out of countenance.

In dark Bolt Court
language lies locked up in folio.
'Confidence' cannot be taken away
and 'Chair ' sleeps easy with its definition:
no slow dissolve in tears and supplications
under that weight of silence. He turns to her:
'Madam, may I assist you – a little tongue?'

A. C. Benson Has a Restless Night

FOR NOEL LLOYD AND GEOFFREY PALMER

Will such pomps and ceremonies never end,
this cavalcade of small pink bricks, and dons
who toss and dip in a cloud of bibbons and ribbons,
those Heads of Houses and their appalling wives
corpulent in fox-furs, bombazine?

'I confess the sight of men in scarlet vexes me
because of the mad and timid joy that flickers in their eyes.'

Broad-beamed faces, settled in their declension,
and a 'Pomeranian dog with its head stuffed with offal,
strange, large flies – grey and tufted,
a sawn-off face dangling from a tree
dropping a horrid, yellow, viscous substance.'

Oh, and those pretty boys with their family airs,
so eager to please m'tutor: Lyttelton, de Grey,
sauntering by, the world, the ball at their feet,
with their cutaway coats, white-collars, centre-partings
and unformed faces stiffening into command.

'Good, earnest, pure, willing –
and I give nearly nothing of myself to them.'

Young men in blood-stained battledress
'and a small, deformed hairy child,
with a curious lower jaw, very shallow:
over the face it had a kind of horny carapace,
made of some material resembling *pottery*'.

Then love's elect, those quick, ingenuous ones
who understand, careless of explanation,
an old man shaken, 'a seal playing with kittens',
our friendships 'flying sun on a bright morning',
Walpole, Mallory, Lubbock, Rylands.

My father the Archbishop, cassocked in purple,
'a grave, commanding, exacting, loving presence'.

And whose pulse beats to this Marche au Supplice?
'I could see his face twitch and grow suddenly pale . . .
he got up and ran to the scaffold, as if glad to be gone.
He was pulled in at one of the swing-doors – a silence.
Then a thing like a black semaphore went down.'

Augustus Hare Considers Another Ghost Story

The plush of these huge trees sags with heat
that weighs more than their tonnage of water;
Through the small tremblings of a pianoforte
servants move as easily as their shadows.
Ladies and gentlemen talk in the flocked light,
make fresh acquaintance with their solitary lives.

It was his mother who was buried alive
and lived for many years afterwards.
It was known she had been put into her coffin
with a very valuable ring upon her finger,

Ah, these old country palaces are choked with mother,
the furious rustling of aunts, adopted, unadopted,
their close-print faces torn from family bibles.
The child who skitters up steps as fast as the flowers
and is whipped for it, talks of the value of rings,
the Taylors, Abruzzo, his work at the Athenaeum.

and the sexton went in after the funeral,
when the coffin was put into the vault, to get it off.
He opened the coffin, but the ring was hard to move,
and he had to rub the dead finger up and down.

Thripps from the harvest-fields creep under glass,
stain clerical uncles crossed in Oxford frames.
Her necklace molten, Lady Campbell tells Madame du
     Quaire
'I always wear a live snake round my throat in hot weather:
it keeps one's neck so cool.' A little laughter,
a little sheet-lightning: frocks paler, greens darkening.

This brought Lady Edgecombe to life, and she sat up.
The sexton fled, leaving the doors of the vault and church open.
Lady Mount Edgecombe walked home in her shroud,
and appeared in front of the windows.

The house at dusk is adrift with beautiful women,
their voices climbing up and down the octave.
A propped head in a carriage bobs by in the Via San Claudio:
that Sicilian Marquis, inhabitant of loss, the Family Spy,
a slim frequenter of tarnished moonlight
looking in from out, watching; once only, speaking.

Those within thought it was a ghost.
Then she walked in at the front door.
When she saw her husband she fainted away in his arms.
This gave her family time to decide what should be done,

In great cool rooms heavy with lilies, he watches
each intransigent face melt into death's brief afterglow.
Insistent, insistent – 'What? Where? Whither?
These questions sometimes hold me breathless.'
Does the creator demand the sacrifice of his creature?
Because he loves his cat, Selma, Aunt Edith hangs it.

and they settled to persuade her
it had been a terrible delirium.
When she recovered from her faint, she was in her own bed,
and she ever after believed it had been a dream.

His mother, 'beyond measure disgusted', gives him away;
as the house fills with the chirping of thousands of crickets
his adopted mother, his darling, dies in his arms
with camellias, her bronze wolf, hymn books, little gold tray.
The only words his father ever speaks to him are
'Good little Wolf: good little Wolf.'

The Healer of Sick Pearls

(Kipling's Kim refuses to be hypnotised by Lurgan Sahib.
The broken remains broken; Kim's vision remains his own)

In the House of The Healer of Sick Pearls
devil-masks in frowst and slashed vermilion
peer through bolt on bolt of clothy stuff
scribbled with maze and golden indirection,
while voices nesting in his phonograph
make tuneless plaint of distance, dust and wax.
He floats a jug of water from his hand
which comes to rest on uncreased napery
white as that innocence once claimed for you
by tracts of garden green and crooked wigwams
for noble savages. Look at it closely.
The fired earth curves about the well of self
through which an oil lamp crazy paves the water
with tiny hieroglyphs and half-built faces.
'Now, throw it back!'

        Take it in both hands,
that dark skull throbbing over sick lightning,
and toss it aimlessly. Look, from the lip
and lazy gape, they all come sprawling:
a Palladian bridge breaks to its reflection,
scabbed urinals in a barrack block
gather their sluicing, hissing act together,
the child's toboggan shrieks into a drift
and all goes falling, falling in slow motion
while the room sobs, and all the pictures tousle.
The spectrum dies to nothing but the stain
of some slight threadbare murder on the carpet,
and little bits of gone, and gone for ever
conglobulate and rock in sparkling potsherds,

an unprovisioned fleet which lies at anchor,
scuttled by sun-glow.

                    His fingers crawl
warm at your nape. 'Look carefully,
nothing is lost, the form will not be lost,
watch how it grows, makes itself whole again.
From dust, the drowsy tilt and sway of things,
the pieces move in their attraction,
kiss and click and climb into a jigsaw
which holds the children in their cosy duffles
hauling the sled back up the snowing hill.
The lovers link their fingers on the bridge
and watch their shaken faces gazing back
from clustered black and silver, soldiers wheel
in sunlight bounced away from badge and buckle:
the old light new, and laddering the deep
unsteady, steady flux, the potter's clay
spun on a shining wheel till both are one,
the bright container and the thing contained.
See how the last piece slides into its place,
and all completed, as it was . . .'

                        You wrench away.
But it is smashed, smashed. Twice three is six,
and one is seven. Slates pile up arithmetic
in all the humming classrooms of the world;
the dead you loved are cleanly gone to ash.
and have become the chanciness of wind.
an unremarked addition to the sea.
The bridge is down, the lovers lost in rain,
the armouries are locked and Rosebud burns,
the radiant singulars lie banked in cloud.
Why are you here, encased in sliding velvets,
pestered by faces dragging skin from shadow?

The phonograph spills out its cornucopia
of bird-brained voices into greedy moments
which die as darkly as the new ones dapple
a broken tear-flask.

                    It lies as it was thrown.
The glistening clay confirms its fracture;
that voice is yours and yet that voice is his,
the Healer of Sick Pearls who stands behind you,
his test passed and the Great Game begun.

Now that no flaw was found to fault the jewel
it is time to enter the thousands of disguise,
stretch in your skin, feral, and clean-eyed
to distinguish without impediment
the brief, distinct hexameters of snow,
count the paces between bridge and bridge,
rehearse the chosen password, slip the sentries
lounging in unfamiliar uniforms by gates
where children scuff in flimsy anoraks,
note, attentive, but incurious,
how the girl lights her lover's cigarette
then glances down the street with unlit eyes;
how, on the café table, a carafe,
jiggling the light upon your own reflections
holds water pure as a perfected absence.

Name and Nature

One of those things is out there in the wind.
It must be a cry for help,
the help you want to give when the short hairs
shiver, as Housman said,
and you're in hot water, and shaving

much too close to the wind for comfort,
gravelled for words,
the whole divine afflatus
cooling the neck's nape.
Eyes, prickle – but do not cry. For help is at hand,

O cry-for-help, caught between wind and water,
thing that would rather be said than be,
would like to die happy
out in the spell-bound garden,
covered all over in strawberry leaves

by an alphabet whirled in a puzzle of wind
which will not settle for anything less
than a cry for help
answered, as twenty-six letters
change each body terrestrial to one celestial,

though your going, as wind carries you off and away
over the syllable grass
to the syllable loss
is nothing to cry for. 'Help'
is a one word poem, and writ on water.

This Late Tempest

FOR PAT WILLIAMS

> 'Then to the elements
> Be free, and fare thee well.'

Put down the book. Each syllable,
each small, unwearied fleck of shine
drowned in the long grass, will not rust.
As the island forgets them into music,
the text is lost for words,

becomes ground-bass, ground of being,
bears the burden of that song
sung to the loneliness of it all
by faces darkly horned in leaves,
those chopped ribbons of light

the moon balances on the sea.
Whatever has been abjured
or left here glinting for the wind
to hone in its beachcombing
lies patient for discovery

by hopes whose wreck is yet to come
and tongues that cut wild music
back to thickets, plots and dreams again.
Then you, discarnate, a twist
slipped from traps of cloud,

must gather up such substance
as the words, rising, crying,
can dress your absence in.
There – thunder at the sea's sharp rim.
And all begin again.

'Approach, my Ariel, come!'

Some Recent Poetry from Anvil

Heather Buck
Waiting for the Ferry

Nina Cassian
Take My Word for It

Peter Dale
Edge to Edge
SELECTED POEMS

Dick Davis
Touchwood

Carol Ann Duffy
Carol Ann Duffy: The Pamphlet
The World's Wife
LIMITED EDITION
Time's Tidings (ed.)
GREETING THE NEW MILLENNIUM

Martina Evans
All Alcoholics Are Charmers

Michael Hamburger
Collected Poems 1941–1994
Late

Donald Justice
Orpheus Hesitated Beside the Black River
NEW AND SELECTED POEMS 1952–1997

Marius Kociejowski
Music's Bride

Peter Levi
Reed Music

Gabriel Levin
Ostraca

Thomas McCarthy
Mr Dineen's Careful Parade
NEW AND SELECTED POEMS

Stanley Moss
Asleep in the Garden
NEW AND SELECTED POEMS

Dennis O'Driscoll
Weather Permitting
POETRY BOOK SOCIETY RECOMMENDATION

Sally Purcell
Fossil Unicorn

Peter Russell
The Elegies of Quintilius

Ruth Silcock
A Wonderful View of the Sea

Daniel Weissbort
What Was All the Fuss About?